Nurturing Young Catholics

A guide for Confirmation sponsors (and other caring adults)

Joseph Moore

PAULIST PRESS
New York/Mahwah, NJ

Dedication
For David Velasquez

Copyright © 1995 by Joseph Moore

Library of Congress Cataloging-in-Publication Data

Moore, Joseph, 1944-
    Nurturing young Catholics : a guide for confirmation sponsors and other caring adults / Joseph Moore.
        p.   cm.
    Includes bibliographical references.
    ISBN 0-8091-3575-2
    1. Confirmands—Religious life. 2. Teenagers—Religious life. 3. Confirmation—Catholic Church. 4. Catholic Church—Membership. I. Title.
BX935.M66   1995
259´.23´08822—dc20   95-7826
                                                                  CIP

Published by Paulist Press
997 Macarthur Boulevard
Mahwah, NJ 07430

Printed and bound in the
United States of America

Contents

"When I was younger I spoke and thought and reasoned as a child does. But when I became older my thoughts grew far beyond those of my childhood."

1 Corinthians 13:11

"It takes a whole village to raise a child."

African proverb

"Candidates for Confirmation, as for Baptism, fittingly seek the spiritual help of a sponsor..."

Catechism of the Catholic Church
Part Two: 1311

Introduction

I'm writing this booklet because I find many adults today are thrust into the role of Confirmation sponsor by the request of a teenager and often have very little understanding of their role. I'm also writing it for other adults, perhaps CCD teachers, or youth group leaders, or friends of someone's parents who have a young person turn to them for guidance. I'm not writing it for any particular Confirmation programs which often have their own set of sponsor expectations. I'm writing it to help adult Catholics feel more secure about what it is they are perhaps being asked to do in a Confirmation. I'm trying to provide a few simple guidelines for you when you're dealing with religious questions or developmental problems and crises of adolescence. I don't have all the answers, but I hope my suggestions which come out of thirty years of my own youth ministry experience will be of some help to you. Accompany your reading of this booklet with prayer that the Spirit of Jesus will lead this young Catholic along the path to life because of (or in spite of!) the accompaniment on the journey which you offer.

I just want to note that I haven't written here for parents, at least of their own children. The role of parent as standards-setter and boundary-keeper is not the same as being an adult friend to a youth. An adult friend is able to be much more accepting of behavior, non-judgmental and permissive of behavior than a parent can (or, more importantly, ought to) be. So if you're a parent of teenagers reading this, apply these suggestions more to someone else's teenage children.

1. What Is Mentoring the Young About?

Mentoring is an art slipping away from society. When I was young I wasn't raised by just my parents, but by the entire town in which I lived. If I was misbehaving, I was scolded by the nearest adult. How different life is today. People who live in neighborhoods seem so isolated from their neighbors. The friends or even acquaintances folks have no longer seem based at all on physical proximity. There's a new attitude across the land which sounds something like "mind your own business." In my parish, a parent recently complained to the pastor that another parishioner asked her child (who was with his friends) to be quiet during Mass; she was outraged that another adult had taken the responsibility of correcting her child. Can you see what a shift this attitude is in society? And as for teenagers, forget it! Most people don't dare to admonish kids over the age of twelve, fearing for their own safety or property. Last summer I very nicely asked a group of teenage girls to be quiet during a movie—they were seated in front of us. Instead of embarrassment and silence, I was confronted with an obscene gesture and the accompanying expletives!

Mentoring, or the art of guiding the young, used to happen automatically in society. This is obviously no longer true. And so to fill up this vacuum, we need adults who are willing to form *intentional* relationships with young people for short-term commitments (or longer ones) depending upon the role. If you're a Confirmation sponsor, then whether you realize it or not you're in the role of a mentor.

As a Confirmation program director, I've seen a lot of sponsors who are quite awkward about their role. The starting point is to realize that you mean something special in the eyes of this teenager. (By the way, everything that is said in this pamphlet applies to *anyone* who has a young person turn to him or her for guidance whether that is explicitly stated or not.) Even if you don't even know this teenager, you obviously have some sort of attraction as a human being for him or her. Even if the teenager is someone you know intimately (like a sibling) and even have a lot of conflicts with, still, at some profound level, this young person is looking up to you.

So start out by trusting in and digesting the fact that you are significant in this kid's eyes. He or she gave your name to the program director or wrote it down on an index card for some reason. The young person may not even be able to articulate or explain the reason. That doesn't matter. It could be instinctual recognition of your goodness or excellence in these young eyes. Enjoy the fact! Don't slough it off or put it down. Of course sometimes we don't like accepting this reality because it implies a responsibility of trying to live up to standard at which we are being held. It means trying to be authentic, to "walk it like we talk it." This is the challenge implicit in being a Confirmation sponsor or in being a Christian adult to whom a young person looks up. But it's a wonderful challenge, and it will help you to grow in human and spiritual maturity (there's really no difference between these two types of maturity) at the same time as you help this young person to grow.

It might be stretching it to say you're a hero, but some of you are to these kids. We're also undergoing a societal shift in terms of our definition of heroes. A hero used to be a figure far off whom we admired and emulated. But for the youth of today, so many heroes have fallen off their pedestals that a real credibility gap has set in. How many athletes, music idols, politicians, and other celebrities have turned out to be very inauthentic people whose behavior in their private lives has been nothing to admire let alone copy! There's a sad cynicism already in the hearts of teenagers about whom they can look up to because just about every one of them has been betrayed by some celebrity they once idolized.

But maybe it's not so bad that the media expose the private lives of public figures today in a way that never happened in years gone by. Maybe this will mean that children and young people will have to look for heroes within their own circle of relationships since we can no longer trust in the stature of people we don't really know personally. A role, such as being an athlete, is no longer a guarantee that this person possesses a certain code of moral values. But the adults they do know personally can't escape the scrutiny for authenticity, integrity and commitment. My hunch about heroism is that it's moving to the local level. More than ever before, kids are looking for adults who are selfless, faith-filled, and completely genuine. Don't sell yourself short. They may even be looking to you. It isn't the role you have, it's the honesty you exude. Heroes for the future will be, in a sense, nobodies, not celebrities—"nobodies" like Jesus.

2. If We're Nurturing Young Catholics, What Is a Catholic Identity?

While they're surely superficial as related to a Catholic identity, engrained deep in my being are the following memories: incense, Tantum Ergo, beeswax, the smell of the bath powder of my first grade teaching nun when she swept by my desk in a mystical way with her mysterious layers of cloth and those long rosary beads, flowers at Forty Hours, ashes on my forehead in the grocery store and an inner swelling of pride over John F. Kennedy. There are a thousand shapes and sounds and smells that are deep in my gut that taught me who I was: a Roman Catholic. While these are my "identity triggers," if you're under the age of forty they might be things like the kindness of somebody's mom who was a CCD teacher, the friendliness felt around church, the intensity of hugs and tears on retreats, religious folk music, the look in the eyes of the old people at the nursing home or of the homeless at the soup kitchen where you did your service program for Confirmation.

This is one level of what some mean by "Catholic identity." Others seem to mean by "Catholic identity" an intellectual grasp of Church doctrine and practice: knowing what the Immaculate Conception means, the seven sacraments, the liturgical seasons and so on. When some adults lament the "loss" of Catholic identity they are referring to the lack of intellectual knowledge of young people of fundamental Catholic theology as well as Catholic tradition. And still others refer to a loss of Catholic identity when a young person possesses a rather vague sense of being a Christian without any apparent appreciation of his or her unique Catholic tradition and culture. What I would like to do is to attempt to discuss a "Catholic" identity of the young—what it can be and what it ought not to be.

In its most limited sense, Catholic identity refers to the institution of the Church wanting to perpetuate itself through the affiliation of the young. This isn't wrong, it's simply limited. Out of this the question emerges whether it is better or worse to first have an identity as a Christian and secondarily to identify with the community in which one lives out one's Christianity? I recall several visits I have made to the Taizé community in France where thousands of young people flock in pilgrimage. When it is announced that one Communion line is for the "Lutheran" or Protestant Eucharist and the other Communion line is for the Roman Catholic, it seems by my observation to make very little difference to the young people there. They simply fall into line where logistically it is convenient, at least for the most part. This is a clear symbol of the lack of concern teens and young adults have about the difference among Christians. Maybe drawing less circles around ourselves is the movement of the Spirit in the churches. So Catholic identity isn't clinging to your own tradition and practice; rather a truly "Catholic" identity implies openness to truth and religious experience wherever we uncover it and at the *same* time treasuring your own heritage.

Now you hear a lot of Catholic adults complaining today that Catholic teens in Confirmation programs "don't know anything." I would ask what is it that they need to know. Do they know that Jesus is Lord and that he lives and that someday we too shall live with him forever? Do they know that loving God and loving neighbor are the heart of the Christian life? Do they know Jesus through the breaking of the bread at Mass? Do they realize the Gospel values of sharing and simplicity? Do they feel the need for prayer and do they know how to pray? Do they know they are responsible for their brothers and sisters in society, throughout the world? Do they know that God will forgive them when they fall and sin? If they know these things, they know a great deal. It's more important that they meet Jesus in the Eucharist more than it is to memorize the seven sacraments or Apostles' Creed (even though I would expect them to commit these to memory). I would rather that they live the beatitudes than be able to recite the Ten Commandments or the precepts of the Church. If they attend a Catholic high school we might expect a better grasp of theology and Catholic tradition. But if they don't, can't we be content with a minimal grasp of Church doctrine? I want to be sure that they are in love with Jesus Christ, with themselves, with others, with the oppressed, with the Eucharist and with the Scriptures. I want to know where their hearts are. This seems to be the concern of Jesus as he evangelized and catechized the "religiously illiterate" of his day. Attitudes and behavior ranked higher than intellectual understanding or knowledge of the Jewish law.

We need to turn to psychology if we're going to use the word "identity" or talk about a Catholic identity. Erik Erikson is the one who wrote so much about adolescence as the time of identity formation—or, to put it simply, figuring out who you are. Of course, we do this our whole lives. Right now you're trying to figure out who you are as a sponsor or a mentor for a young person. But even though it's an endless task, there's some fundamental life experience that's supposed to happen when you're young if you are to grow and develop as a person. Erikson says identity is achieved through intimacy—not sexual intimacy, which is today's limited meaning of this word. He's talking about psychological intimacy where you let at least one other human being in on who you really are by sharing your honest thoughts, fears, shame, doubts, and so on. If you can find acceptance for your complete self, even this "dark side," Erikson says this will lead to self-acceptance which is how you solidify who you are. Erikson is pretty accurate, so let's use his approach to identity as a starting place to discuss Catholic identity.

I want to suggest that the way a young Catholic gets Catholic identity is to have an experience of the parish which is one of intimacy. The experience of intimacy is first of all one of unconditional acceptance and love. And secondly, it is one that ties my own identity to the mind of Jesus Christ. Before we discuss this second aspect of the intimacy experience let's talk about the parish as the focus of the intimacy experience.

Youth ministry leaders in this country have long been telling local churches that the parish needs to be more welcoming to the young. The typical teenager standing in the vestry, on the edge of the congregation, has symbolized the struggle youth leaders have had in turning Sunday worship into a place of hospitality. Youth ministry is the ministry of the entire church. Youth ministry is the responsibility of the entire parish, just as raising a child is the responsibility of an entire community.

And in an eloquent article, "Parish as Catechist," theologian Tom Groome remarks:

> ...all people should find in their local parish a truly "Catholic" community a place of welcome and inclusion, where all can feel a sense of belonging and of being "at home." Faith development researchers say that young people have an even greater felt need for a sense of "belonging" to their parish than do adults; they also warn that many congregations fail particularly in this regard. Interviews with young people who have "left the church" often reveal that many don't feel they have left, but that they *never* belonged. (From "Parish as Catechist in Church," Fall, 1990, Vol. 6, Number 3, p. 25.)

Actually as a sponsor or mentor you are a part of this experience of welcome and acceptance. Your own non-judgmental
(which is not to be confused with non-challenging) posture
toward such teenagers is absolutely crucial if they are to find in
the Catholic Church a place to belong where they feel loved
for who they are.

3. *Identity in Christ*

We have been saying that young persons first discover their Catholic identity through a welcoming faith community which invites them in and helps them to find a place within the Church and be accepted and loved for who they are—which, when you think about it, mirrors the unconditional love of God. And the second part of the intimacy experience is that along with the love and acceptance is the invitation to grow to spiritual maturity. This takes into account Jesus as a challenger as well as a comforter. If I've been able to be vulnerable enough to expose my real self to the community, the first step in my healing is the acceptance of others. But a second step is for that community to share with me its collective wisdom about where truth lies and happiness is found. This is also a part of forming a Catholic identity. All too many adults would like to skip over the acceptance experience and move into the challenges. This is a mistake because it fails to acknowledge our make-up as social human beings. Another mistake we adults sometimes make is to think that we can preach to kids about the challenges of Catholic Christianity and leave it at that. But it's back to that old adage of credibility: "Walk it like you talk it!"—and there isn't much that teenagers miss today in terms of hypocrisy.

"At root, the problem of the evangelization of youth is not that they have not had a chance to *hear* the message. The problem is that they have found all too few believable

groups of Christians *living* it," says religious educator
Michael Warren. (From "Youth Evangelization and
Counter Evangelization," *The Living Light*, Fall, 1993, p.
51.)

In other words, we're back to the notion that faith isn't
"taught" but "caught," and to the newer concept that the adult
with faith isn't a "sage on the stage" but a "guide on the side."
Faith isn't passed from generation to generation through
schooling or CCD but rather through a faith-filled community.
Young people know the wisdom of the Church in moral matters not so much by our telling as by our living. It's *our* appreciation of human sexuality and personal commitment; it's *our*
own unwillingness to cheat or live a lie; it's *our* simplicity of
lifestyle and lack of greed; it's *our* forgiveness and respect within our families; it's *our* own actions on behalf of the persecut-
ed, the poor and the powerless—it's these that teach the young
about the challenge Jesus Christ offers us to grow into spiritual
adulthood. I receive an identity not only from what others tell
me about myself, but also from observing the lives of significant people around me. And that, my friend, my Confirmation
sponsor, includes you!

To conclude, let me simply say that there is a place for learning about the teachings and tradition of the Catholic faith. But
this is secondary to the formation of a Catholic identity. This
identity is formed through an experience called "intimacy"—intimacy involving being both accepted by the community and
also invited by the community to become all that I can be. Does
this de-emphasize Church teaching and give priority to living life
in a particular way (attitudes and behavior)? I suppose so, but
let's not conclude that doctrine isn't important. It's a matter of
emphasis. I side with Walt Whitman who said: "A morning glory
at my window satisfies me more than the metaphysics of
books." That sounds like something Jesus would say too. (Walt
Whitman, "Song of Myself," stanza 24.)

4. So Where Does Prayer Fit In?

We just said that Jesus is both a challenger and a comforter, and we talked about embodying these challenges in our own lives as Catholic adults. So now let's talk about Jesus as our source of strength and courage and healing.

In a society of upheaval and change where family life in its traditional forms is breaking down, we are inheriting a generation in need of stability, of something secure, of someone to believe in. And we adults have the graced opportunity to point them toward Jesus. The language of the psalms which calls God our refuge and our fortress is very appropriate today. Unfortunately many young people put their trust in illusions like sex or fame or power or riches. But they burn through these experiences early. I know several young adults in their late twenties who are reclaiming their virginity. They have slept around in their youth, but their hunger for intimacy hasn't been filled. There are "yuppies" who have the condo, the BMW and the sailboat who are now asking: "Isn't there something more?" And how many famous celebrities in our time, having achieved fame and stature, have chosen a path of self-destruction!

Prayer or communication with God is essential for young people to practice if they're going to walk through life with any inner peace. Many sponsors and nurturing adults feel awkward about the dimension of prayer in their role with a teenager. The Catholic culture for a long time has looked at prayer as a very private matter. Even when we worship together at Mass, many

people still are in their own "private world" and only acknowledge the existence of those around them during the sign of
peace. Also as Catholics we're not used to talking about our
lives of prayer or in sharing prayer openly with another individual. So if you feel a little uptight about talking to teens about
prayer, try to realize that your feelings are very understandable
given the religious culture in which we were raised. And add to
that, if you're a male, that your gender hasn't been taught by
the culture to share openly about interior feelings like a life of
prayer in God.

So you may need to take a risk to help a teenager appreciate
the value of prayer in your life. It might be a good idea to share
just how and when you pray, your difficulties in prayer, and also
the benefits prayer has offered you. Prayer is very personal
because it is the communication of our heart's deepest long-
ings; such communication is a two-way street of listening and
speaking. I'm going to make a few suggestions from my own
experience with young people about ways that might help
them see prayer in new ways and therefore grow into a spiritual adulthood.

Six Tips for Teens on Prayer

✍ See prayer as asking. Prayer is definitely a way to access
the grace and goodness of God by asking God to help us
in all the various circumstances of life. I strongly recom-
mend that "prayer of petition" among teenagers be
encouraged, especially since they are in such a self-cen-
tered period of life. They need a few cautions such as:

▶ Bring to God your deepest needs and those of others,
but save your selfish or materialistic concerns for your
own energy.

▶ Remember that God helps those who help themselves.

Accompany your prayer with courageous human effort to attain the things for which you pray.

▶ Don't be superstitious in prayer. The miracle of life is that God's Spirit moves all of the time in the ordinary and very seldom in the extraordinary. Don't waste time looking for God in places God seldom goes.

▶ Be persistent—remember the story in Luke's Gospel of the man who finally got up in the night to answer the door because he became tired of the continuous knocking.

▶ Try to realize that sometimes prayer changes us instead of changing situations. Sometimes we are praying for something we think we want, but God knows best.

▶ Don't feel the need to defend God or explain the inexplicable when prayers seem not to be answered. Clichés like "God must know best" are quite unhelpful. Prayer is a relationship, and like all love affairs there is a trust that needs to build over a period of many years.

✍ Help kids to use the Bible, especially the Gospel. They don't need to know the Bible extensively, nor do you. But it is a real gift to teach yourself and to teach a teenager how to take a little section of a Gospel like a parable or a story of one of Jesus' cures and to read it slowly with a vivid imagination—and then to close the Scriptures and think about how these few lives apply to your life, what they say to you personally.

✍ Teach young people how to be quiet for a few minutes. Many of them live in music constantly and can also pray with music and other noises. But they also need to learn that prayer isn't just asking and talking, but also listening to God's voice in the stillness of our hearts. I suggest to kids that they shut out noise and either close their eyes or focus on an object like a candle or crucifix for just three minutes. (By the way three minutes can be a very long time if you have no inner discipline of silence.) I invite them to try to get into this practice of clearing their mind's clutter for a few minutes each day so they can experience Christ's presence within their hearts. To reverse a cliché I say: "Don't just do something; sit there!"

✎ Encourage them to pray in ways they find best. Some like being out in nature, others like to listen to meaningful music, and some like to lie on their beds and look at the ceiling. Whatever works is OK. God doesn't really care when or how we turn our hearts to prayer and acknowledge God's presence within us.

✎ Talk about the Eucharist and what a beautiful and sacred gift it is. An old Baptist saying goes: "Better felt than telt." That's how it is with the Eucharist. Lessons in theology or CCD about the meaning of the Eucharist add little to a person's spirituality without the regular experience of receiving this treasure, this sacrament, physically into our beings. If they receive Holy Communion on a regular basis they will experience the unfolding mystery of Jesus Christ in their hearts and souls.

✎ Don't be defensive when Sunday liturgy is criticized. My feelings are that kids are often right. Why should Mass be boring? Good liturgy that relates well to those celebrating isn't boring. The quality of preaching may be poor or the music may not move them. Unfortunately, many parishes still don't know how to celebrate a liturgy that both welcomes young people and touches them deeply. I have given up trying to defend liturgy done poorly. We go to

God, after all, through the human. That's what we are—we have no other path. What I can do is to suggest to groups of young people that they mobilize to work on better liturgy themselves in conjunction with parish staffs and committees. Sometimes I suggest to an individual that he or she seek out a liturgy in the geographical area which does meet his or her human and spiritual needs.

5. Let's Look at the Family

If you befriend or sponsor a teenager, it's impossible to look at him or her in isolation from the family of origin. Most of the trouble spots in the lives of adolescents (like chemical dependency, eating disorders, depression, violence, and so on) can be traced to some kind of dynamic within the family. I'm not suggesting that as a caring adult you need to be a family therapist! I'm just saying that you need to remember there is a huge backdrop to the life of this young person.

There is no such thing as a perfect family. All families, whether there are two parents or one or a guardian, have problems. Families are also "systems" which means that family members are emotionally connected together. If the relationships are right, then the system works well. If one of the members isn't functioning properly (e.g. if a parent is an alcoholic) then the entire family system is impacted. A teenager may need to talk with you about a family problem as a part of your role. Be open to that possibility. Every teenager needs an adult (and I include young adults) to help him or her sort out life as it is happening during those crucial years. Sometimes one encounters parents who are insecure in their own lives (and hence their relationship with their teen is shaky) or who want to hide some family secret and who may feel threatened by the friendship between their son or daughter and a special adult. If this is the case, try to keep communication with parents open and ongoing without, of course, revealing any confidences their child has shared. And also too there can be parents who are so immature themselves that they become jealous of your relationship with their teenager. In this instance, there is really little you can do to change the adult. Time will probably teach them that your guidance of their daughter or son has actually enhanced their own relationship with their child.

Family "secrets" occur when a family denies a problem, and then the secret becomes a problem. I'll use the example of chemical dependency again since it is such a prevalent problem—about twenty-five percent of teenagers in this country are affected by a family member who uses drugs or alcohol. Another family secret can be abuse: physical, sexual, or verbal or any combination of these. When teenagers live with secrets in the family system they turn to unhealthy behaviors for survival. A word to describe this phenomenon is "co-dependency." When a young person feels shame, confusion, betrayal, and other negative feelings, the tendency is to internalize these feelings and then to choose coping mechanisms which dull the pain the feelings generate. Some examples are drug use and compulsive addictions: to food, working out, sex, criminal activity—a wide range of addictions. When you see an unhealthy behavior pattern in teenagers, you know that it's only the tip of the iceberg. Such kids need to talk about what's going on not only within them but also at home. The first step is for them to overcome the denial about what's really going on—what's happening in the family and also what their own compulsive behavior is doing to them. You may or may not be the adult these youths open up to. You may not have the competence to deal with the problem presented, but you can encourage them to talk to a counselor at school, or to a trusted family member, or perhaps to seek therapy. You can also encourage them to go to a group like Alateen which provides emotional support for children of alcoholics. There is also a support group called CoDa—Teen. To find out if there is a group in your area write P.O. Box 33577, Phoenix, AZ 85067-

3577 or call (602) 277-7991. Other "hot line" numbers appear at the end of this section.

Just letting teenagers talk about their life, their concerns, is a beautiful gift. In our frantic age, many parents do not give their children sufficient time to unload their thoughts and feelings. It is, after all, by talking out loud—about who they think they are—that young persons can finally figure out who they really are. And when dealing with unhealthy behaviors that you observe in a young person, you have done a service just by naming them. Saying the words breaks the silence. Even if these young persons are too insecure or not yet ready to deal with what they need to confront, the simple fact that you have observed and named something is probably the opening that they needed to one day face what needs to be faced. So often in ministry with teenagers we are sowing seeds that we personally will never see come to blossom.

Other Helpful Resources

Runaways

Covenant House Nineline	800-999-9999
National Runaway Hotline	800-231-6946
(in Texas)	800-392-3352

Suicide   617-247-8050

    (in Massachusetts and New Hampshire)   800-252-8336

Abuse

Child Help USA	800-4-A-CHILD
Incest Survivors Anonymous	213-428-5599

Chemical Dependency

Al-Ateen	800-356-9996
(in New York)	800-245-4656
National Institute on Drug Abuse	800-662-HELP
Narcotics Anonymous	818-780-3951

Eating Disorders

Overeaters Anonymous	213-542-8386

Anorexics/Bulimics Anonymous (for support group info write: P.O. Box 112214, San Diego, CA 92111).

Gambling (for Gam-A-Teen support groups for teens whose families are impacted by gambling write: Gamblers Anonymous, P.O. Box 17173, Los Angeles, CA 90017).

6. Some Trouble Spots

It's no news flash that in today's society many young people engage in "risky" behaviors such as drug/alcohol use, attempted suicide and sexual activity. I want to introduce you in this section to a wonderful study called "The Troubled Journey: A Profile of American Youth." It looks at almost fifty thousand students in grades 6–12, gathering a composite of attitudes and behaviors.

Some bad news from the study is that the older that teenagers are, there is an increase in the likelihood that they are involved in risky behaviors. Another disturbing result is the statistic that one-third of girls in grades 10–12 reported at least one incident of physical and/or sexual abuse, which in turn more than doubles the chances of depression, stress and low self-esteem. The "at risk" behaviors fall more or less into one of these categories:

- alcohol use;
- smoking cigarettes;
- use of illegal drugs;
- depression;
- attempted suicide;
- fighting;
- vandalism/theft;
- weapon use;
- school absenteeism/drop out;

▶ drinking and driving;

▶ bulimia (an eating disorder).

There's an old saying that grace builds on nature. Another way to put it is that this young person for whom you are a sponsor or "mentor" or friend may be involved in some risky behaviors given the culture in which we live. After twenty-five years of youth ministry, I find it's safer for me to presume risky behavior rather than the alternative of presuming that risky behaviors are not occurring. If you're under the age of thirty you probably would think that anyway. If you're over thirty and don't have any wide-ranging contact with kids (except your own perhaps) you might be just a little naive about what goes on in the contemporary teenage subculture. All I'm suggesting is that risky behavior of some sort is a real possibility.

Now the study went on to discover that there are ten liabilities or deficits which, when they are present, make risky behavior, not automatic, but much more likely. In rank order of prevalence these ten deficits are:

1. Student spends two or more hours per day at home without an adult (58%);

2. Student places high importance on self-serving values (48%);

3. Student watches TV three or more hours per day (40%);

4. Student frequently attends parties where peers drink (31%);

5. Student feels under stress or pressure "most" or "all" of the time (21%);

6. Student reports at least one incident of physical abuse by an adult (17%);

7. Student reports at least one incident of sexual abuse (10%);

8. Student reports a parent "has a serious problem with drugs or alcohol" (7%);

9. Student feels a consistent lack of care, support, and understanding (6%);

10. Most close friends are involved in chemical use and/or are in frequent trouble at school (2%).

The percentages given here are based on the grades 6–12. For individual grade differences as well as differences between male and females you would need to look at the entire study.

Now on the other side of the coin, there are a number of "assets" or factors promoting positive teenage development. As you would suspect, the more assets in the life of a young person, the more equipped he or she is to make good choices and avoid risky behaviors. I'm not going to list all the assets the study points to (there are thirty in all), but following are some that may interest you in your special role:

▶ family support;
▶ parent communication;
▶ other adult resources (that's you!);
▶ other adult communication (that's you!);
▶ positive school climate;
▶ time at home;
▶ positive peer influence;
▶ involved in church or synagogue;
▶ values helping people;
▶ is concerned about world hunger;
▶ cares about people's feelings;
▶ values sexual restraint;

▶ self-esteem;
▶ positive view of personal future.

Can you see how much impact you can have in the life of a teenager? First of all, just having you to talk with is an asset. Secondly, whatever you might say, model or encourage can be an asset. If you're involved in a Confirmation program, that itself is an asset. And just by your acceptance of this young person you're building self-esteem which is yet another asset. Don't sell yourself short. Who you are, how you interact, what you do and say can be extremely powerful in the life of a teenager. I know it's not usually apparent, but how many times as a teacher and youth minister I've had kids come back to me and say: "Remember when you said...?" or "Remember when this happened..." Half the time I've forgotten what I said or did, but obviously this other person didn't. As Jesus said, the fields are ripe for the harvest. It's just that you may not still be around in the life of this young person when the harvest comes in and he or she moves off into independence.

The last piece of data I'd like to point out is that some youths tend to thrive despite the social deficits in their lives. These "thrivers" tend to come from positive family dynamics and *other systems of support.* Deficits are not destiny. You and I can make a difference. Sometimes we can even *be* the difference.

For more information about this study,

"The Troubled Journey"
Contact:
RespecTeen
Lutheran Brotherhood
625 Fourth Avenue, So.
Minneapolis, MN 55415

7. A Word About Sex and Sexuality

I want to say a little bit about sex and sexuality. It's a burning issue in adolescence because it has so much to do with figuring out who you are. David Elkind, an expert on adolescence in his book, *All Grown Up and No Place to Go*, says that for some teenagers not to have had sexual intercourse can contribute to low self-esteem and feelings of inadequacy. This would emanate out of the misconception that everyone is having sex who is in one's peer teen group. And this is not the case. Gallup surveys have said that about 50% of teens have had intercourse at least once before high school graduation, while "The Troubled Journey" study found that 77% of boys and 66% of girls in Grade 12 had had intercourse at least once. Yet, other studies report a recent decline in sexual activity among teens, citing the scare of AIDS and other factors.

Whatever the real statistics are, don't be too naive about the prevalence of sexual activity among teenagers. I see several reasons for this: "Adolescence" lasts longer—or at least marriage is often postponed until a couple has completed their studies or become established in their careers; the prevalence of birth control has weakened the traditional support for abstinence (although birth control methods among teens are only used about half of the time, and also condoms are often used improperly); low self-esteem propels kids into sex in order to feel valued—and this is also related to the high incidence of teen pregnancy where a young woman has a baby to reinforce her own self-worth; lack of parental supervision in the home;

media bombardment of sexual messages; the frequent use of alcohol and other drugs by teens; and the failure of many parents to set clear boundaries for their children. These are some of my own hunches about why this generation of young people is so sexually active. And add to all this that, given the level of violence today, many kids wonder if they will be around to enjoy the sex they are supposed to delay. A decade or two ago, it was the threat of nuclear destruction that contributed to an immediacy among teens; today it's the threat of personal destruction by a gun or knife. Just about every recent poll of the worries of teenagers puts the threat of violence at the top of the list.

So what are you to do, sponsor, mentor, in the face of these huge societal issues? Well, you can start with being open to what young folks choose to share with you on this topic. This implies that you're comfortable enough in your own body with your own sexuality if you're going to listen to the sexual exploits and heartaches of teenagers. Secondly, don't be judgmental. If you show the least bit of shock, disapproval, or anger, you will be immediately turned off. You do not need to condone behaviors, but you have to let these kids know you accept them as they are. You can gently challenge to abstinence even if an experience of lost virginity is confided to you. Young people need to know that virginity can be spiritually reclaimed. They also need to know that they have support from wise people like you so that they don't feel pressured to get involved sexually with someone to whom they cannot yet commit their lives. Many successes are being reported when young people band together to publicly pledge to chastity. The National Federation of Catholic Youth Ministry promotes a wonderful program of sex education entitled "True Love Waits" (for more information on this program contact your own diocesan youth ministry office). Positive peer pressure is just as powerful as negative peer pressure.

I remember Ben, a sixteen year old boy who came to me to

discuss whether or not his junior prom should be his first experience of sexual intercourse. From that conversation and many like that I offer to you the following suggestions when you deal one on one in a pastoral role (like a Confirmation sponsor) on issues of sex and sexuality.

1. Don't be judgmental—conceal any surprise or shock as best you can;

2. Accept the individual;

3. Challenge the behavior or invite the teen to restraint for greater goals if that's what needs to be done;

4. Discuss abstinence as a daily decision as opposed to a long-range commitment which often seems overwhelming to a young person;

5. Share as much of your own life experience and insights as you feel able and as is appropriate.

Before we leave this topic, I want to share with you some other refreshing insights from "The Troubled Journey" study relative to sexual activity. Who are the teenagers faithful to the values of their parents and their church?

▶ They are those who have been *taught* that abstinence is a value;
▶ They are those who tend to be *involved* in their churches;
▶ They are involved and achieve as a high school student.

Lastly, I want to touch upon the fact that not all teenagers are heterosexual, that a small percentage of them are gay and lesbian. Now many teenagers have anxiety over homosexual experience or fantasies and sometimes all you need to do is to assure them that this is normal during the sexual burgeoning of adolescence and that thoughts and even experiences don't define one as necessarily homosexual. But there are those whose orientation is clearly not heterosexual and they know that about themselves. A recent Federal Department of Health and Human Services report on teen suicide stated that gay and lesbian youth were two to three times more likely to attempt suicide than heterosexual teenagers! They are also more likely to suffer clinical depression and substance abuse problems, and they make up forty percent of all homeless youths. A 1989 federal study indicated that thirty percent of completed teenager suicides involve sexual orientation conflicts. What does all this data say to us pastorally as the Church of Jesus Christ? We have to begin by saying the word "homosexual" or its equivalents in Catholic circles. We can't pretend that these young people who are so in need of ministry are not there. Just as I urged you not to be naive about sexual activity, I'd invite you not to be naive about this matter either. Sometimes by just naming the reality or asking the right question as you try to get at the roots of a kid's depression gives permission for a teenager to open up.

Here's a wonderfully insightful statement on "casual" sex, so dominant in the youth culture of today. It's written a little over the heads of teenagers, but maybe if you digest it yourself you'll find a way of sharing its insights with your teenage friend.

> The problem with casual sex is that keeping sex casual is difficult. A couple may come together determined simply to have an enjoyable sexual relationship. "We like each other and want to give each other pleasure," they avow, "but with 'no strings attached.'" They agree on this limited arrangement, but the experience develops differently. Beyond their plans, even against their conscious ambitions, they confront the deep issues of sexuality. They find that physical intimacy and psychological intimacy are connected. Sex play reveals more than their bodies; it often uncovers hidden hurts and fragile hopes. In their

lovemaking, more than pleasure is aroused. Sex raises issues of dependence and commitment, even when these matters have been ruled out of bounds. Casual lovers come to admit, "We started out with modest expectations of one another. At first, we just depended on each other to be available when we had agreed—in a good mood, if possible! But our expectations started to expand; it's as though we couldn't help expecting more from each other. We began to look for deeper ways to share our lives with one another. We began to depend on one another for understanding and support, even more than for sex!" *A Sense of Sexuality*, Evelyn Eaton Whitehead and James D. Whitehead, Doubleday, 1989, p. 33.)

8. Finding the Face of the Poor

At the heart of the Christian life is the resurrection of Jesus Christ. As God raised Jesus from the dead, so we too will be raised. But the dying–rising event isn't confined to the end of life. "Dying" and "rising" is the daily experience of Christian living. Matthew's Gospel says it best: "Anyone who finds his life will lose it; anyone who loses his life for my sake will find it" (Matthew 10:39). Paradoxically, we find ourselves by forgetting about ourselves. Jesus moved from power to powerlessness, from success to failure, from glory to shame. He said that anyone who wants to be great among you must be a slave just as the Son of Man came to serve, not to be served (Matthew 20:26–28).

Jesus, you see, shifts the focus to what's really important by dismissing power, fame and riches. The Gospel is replete with images of humility, simplicity and generosity. When young persons are fully initiated into the Catholic Christian community through Confirmation, they are saying at some level that they want to follow this radical path of Jesus. It's radical because it's so opposed to the emphasis in society on getting rich and having power. Of course, teenagers aren't really old enough to have personally experienced that the cravings of the human heart cannot be filled by materialism. Most of us find that out eventually, the hard way. So in a sense the message of Jesus' life makes very little sense to a young person, especially when it's presented in this way, the way that Father Henri Nouwen calls the "path to *downward* mobility" (as opposed to upward). How can you help your Confirmation candidate grasp the fullness of this faith into which he or she is being initiated?

You have little control over young persons' materialistic, hedonistic values. Those have either been pointed to as shallow or else nourished and encouraged in the families from which these kids come. At fourteen or seventeen you are not single-handedly going to alter teenagers' entire value system. But it is possible to open them up a little bit to the values of Jesus. One way is through a community service experience. These are often required as a part of Confirmation preparation. If the service involves people contact with the *poor, oppressed,* or *neglected* in our society, it offers the possibility for genuine discoveries about life's meaning. If the service has no people contact and doesn't expose the teenager to some type of impoverishment it holds very little opportunity to grow.

You see, my theory (which I learned from Gustavo Gutierrez, a Latin American liberation theologian) is that for a person to really know Jesus he or she needs to know at least one poor person on a *personal level*—i.e. have a relationship with that person. Of course there are many kinds of poverty; material, physical (like lacking the use of your legs, or an AIDS diagnosis), societal (like being discriminated against because of your racial or ethnic background) and spiritual (like being elderly and alone in the world or neglected by your family). What kids need to do much more than fundraising and campaigns to address social evils is to have a one-on-one relationship with a person in society who embodies the realities of poverty and powerlessness and perhaps even rejection. In the eyes of this individual is the face of Jesus Christ. We learn from the poor, the disenfranchised what we ourselves are supposed to become as Christians. Many people have been forced into a situation of poverty or discrimination by circumstance. Our poverty is to be a choice where we continually try to simplify our lifestyles by having less for our-selves and sharing more with others. These people are dis-criminated against because of the prejudice in the hearts of narrow-minded people. Our persecution as Christians isn't chosen. But it results from our sticking to the values of Jesus which don't make sense in our selfish society. Especially when we move from *charity* (sharing wealth and doing good for others) to *advocacy* which means fighting for the rights of the poor and powerless do we find ourselves espousing unpopular positions. We may feel very alone and misunder-stood. Of course, that's precisely when we know we are "dying" and "rising" with Jesus. It's when we've "laid down our life" for others in some way that we really discover the beauty of life and the depth of happiness promised in the Gospel—a happiness that far outweighs material pleasures and successes.

This is a tall order to teach all this to the young! How do you do it? Well, one way you *don't* do it is by just preaching about it! Words definitely need to match actions in this arena. If the teenager has had an experience such as I've described, you can help him or her to reflect on it by talking about it. If not, maybe you can have the experience together of reach out. There are so many community agencies (like Catholic Charities, Big Brother, Big Sister, HIV/AIDS service organiza-tions, nursing homes, and homeless shelters) that can offer you the opportunity to have a personal relationship with somebody who is "poor" in some very real way.

Also, the problems of racism and classism and homopho-bia and discrimination (that so dominate our culture and con-tribute to so much violence) are the results of social isolation. When I survey teenagers about the biases they hold, nine times our of ten they have had no friendships with anyone from the group toward which they harbor their prejudices. They see these people as an entity "out there" or "over there." If young persons want to be fully initiated into the mystery of Christ, they need to learn that in Christ all are one, or as St. Paul puts it: "All of you who have been baptized into Christ have clothed yourselves with him. There does not exist among you Jew or Greek, slave or free man, male or female" (Galatians 3:27–28).

9. Some Skills To Listen Better

What follows is a "crash course" in listening skills. So much of "being there" for a teenager is being a good listener. It's by talking with people he or she trusts that a young person figures out their true identity. Listening is a wonderful gift today where everybody seems too busy to listen to kids.

Our problems are a jumble of feelings locked inside us. As we talk out our feelings (hurt, confusion, anxiety, anger, etc.) a good listener functions as a mirror. In other words, by allowing me to talk aloud, a good listener gives me the chance to sort out things by hearing myself speak. Good listening can be a natural gift some people possess, but it can also be a skill that one acquires. A good listener does not daydream, interrupt the speaker, or anticipate what the person is going to say and then jump in to complete the idea. Listening is also an active process where we really try to understand what a speaker is saying.

The first area to be studied and developed in good listening is the helper's non-verbal behavior. This behavior is based on the fact that most of our communication is not in words but in facial expression, body movement, tone of voice, and so on. How often have you, for instance, sensed that someone disapproved of you or your actions even though his or her words indicated otherwise? How often have you known friends who were depressed or upset even though they told you that they were fine? Non-verbal behavior and awareness of it in both ourselves as listeners and in the young person are

35

essential in the helping relationship. The entire time you are listening, your body language, posture, and other non-verbals are conveying something to the listener.

Here are some basic steps to being good listening:

1. **Focus on the speaker:** People need to feel that you are really "with them." This requires blocking out interferences, including the wanderings of your own mind.

2. **Focus on feelings:** Many people hear only words and not the feelings behind what is being said. How often do we avoid the truth and cover our true feelings when someone asks us, "How are you?"

3. **Show understanding:** As a listener, periodically check out what you think is being said. For example, if someone has been telling you about problems with his or her father, you might ask: "You mean you're really afraid of him?" Ask the speaker to clarify for you; this indicates you're listening, as does occasional nodding of your head.

4. **Keep the speaker focused:** Help keep the speaker from wandering off the topic by gently bringing him or her back to the matter at hand. You might say, for example, "Now you were telling me about your feelings toward your father before we got off the track..."

5. **Don't make judgments:** Try to suspend your own values and judgments as persons speak. Rather than saying to yourself, "I disagree with them," spend your energy in trying to listen well so that you can figure out how they came to hold the position they have or took the action that they did.

Responding

Continuing Responses

A continuing response summarizes or reflects the content or feelings presented by the speaker. Continuing responses generally serve two purposes. First, they encourage the person to continue talking. Your words, like your non-verbal behavior, can be encouraging or discouraging. Non-verbally, if you want someone to continue talking, you may occasionally smile or nod your head in agreement or understanding. If you want to stop a conversation, you may frown or look puzzled. Failure to respond verbally can make teens confused and unable to determine whether you understand or care. They will probably stop talking or change the subject. The second purpose of continuing responses is to assist as he or she clarifies the problem. This occurs when the young person "hears" your reflection of the problem just stated.

The most basic continuing response is a "mm-hmm" or "uh-huh" as we convey to the speaker that we are following what is being said. Uttering these simple sounds says, "Go on...I'm listening and understanding." This response, of course, shouldn't be used continually. On the other hand, if you utter nothing for ten minutes while the person talks, he or she will probably think you're a poor listener.

Content responses: A content response summarizes or reflects the content of what the speaker has said. It can summarize the prior statement, several statements made during a conversation, or the entire conversation. By using a content response you act as a "mirror" reflecting back to the person what he or she has just said. These statements should be short and concise. Examples of content responses are:

a) *Teenager:* What a lousy day. My mother yelled at me, my dog got lost, and I got a detention in school.
Helper: You've had a lot to deal with today.

b) *Teenager:* My boyfriend just laughed at me when I said I couldn't dance and then he told all of my friends.

Helper: He thought it was funny, but you didn't.

c) *Teenager:* She just drives me crazy. My blood pressure rises. I scream at everyone.

Helper: She makes you really angry.

Content responses also help people stay on track while they speak. When people talk they tend to ramble, expressing many thoughts at the same time. Content responses not only reassure the speaker that you are listening, but also help him or her to stay focused during the conversation. Look at these examples for beginning a content response:

"You seem to be saying that..."
"If I hear you correctly, you're saying..."
"Correct me if I'm wrong, but you mean that..."
"So, your aim is to..."
"In other words, you want to..."
"Out of all the things that you've said, what seems to be coming through is..."
"From what you've said, it seems to me that..."

Affective Responses: An affective response is a statement in which you, as the listener, reflect a feeling that the speaker has not yet labeled. This response is difficult to make because one must be aware of both the content of the response and the feelings or "affect" felt by the speaker. In other words, you must reach into the content and pull out the feelings.

A helper must listen carefully and be aware not only of what is said, but of how it was said. This presents a greater challenge. The non-verbal behavior and the tone of his or her voice may give clues. More often, though, you have to depend on your own intuition. A helpful technique is to try to imagine how you would feel if the situation being described happened to you. Examples of affective responses are:

a) *Teenager:* I hate my size, I'm so fat...when I walk through school everybody looks at me.
   Helper: You feel embarrassed.
b) *Teenager:* My little brother gets all the attention; my parents favor him. Wherever we go everybody makes a fuss over him because he is supposedly so cute.
   Helper: Sounds like you're a little jealous.
c) *Teenager:* I finally got an "A" in that course. I can't believe it! He never gives an "A"!
   Helper: You're pretty excited.

Very simply, affective responses indicate that we are trying to know what the young person is feeling. While we all have feelings, learning to tune in to feelings and reflecting them accurately takes a lot of practice. It does not come easy. Counselors and psychotherapists work many hours to learn this skill so they can communicate more effectively with their clients.

For many years our society did not encourage the revealing of feelings. Feelings were viewed as being private. There are still some people today who think that a person's feelings should rarely be discussed. Some try to disown them, to deny them, or to distort them for fear that they would reveal some kind of weakness. For too many years the pattern in our society has been to encourage relationships that are distant, formal, and lacking in personal understanding. Many of our problems today are caused by a lack of understanding of our own feelings. Hiding our feelings is a step on the road to emotional illness.

The Art of Questioning

Questions are another way of responding to someone, but asking questions is not as easy as it might seem. To ask questions appropriately is a real skill. Bombarding people with a lot of questions can make them feel defensive and uneasy. At the outset of a helping interaction, questions are appropriate to gain understanding of the situation. If a teenage girl says, "My father went nuts on us again this morning," you might need to ask something like, "What do you mean 'nuts'? What did he do?" You need to know if she is talking about verbal or physical abuse, drunkenness, or a mental imbalance. You are entitled to sufficient information to grasp the problem.

Remember, however, that there is a difference between necessary questions and nosy, unnecessary ones. There is no place for a nosy helper. For example, if the girl answers, "Well, he hit me and then he hit my mother before he left for work," you have enough information. But if you ask questions like, "Did your mother bleed? Did she get a bruise? Did she hit him back?" you are being nosy. Those questions don't pertain directly to the problem. They come from curiosity, not a desire to be helpful.

Open and Closed Questions

Questions can be categorized as open or closed. An open question encourages a person to develop an answer and talk at greater length and in more detail than with a closed question. The closed question generally calls for a simple "yes" or "no," and it is typically phrased so that the answers are limited to a few words. The following examples indicate the difference between open and closed questions:

Do you get along with your parents? (closed)
What can you tell me about your relationship with your parents? (open)
Do you like school? (closed)
How do you feel about school? (open)
Are you going to call her again? (closed)
What do you think you'll do now? (open)

The open question encourages the person to share more feelings and thoughts. It is a way of probing that is not nosy but helpful because it encourages the person to talk more. Closed questions are more appropriate when you need to gather information.

Asking "Why?"

Generally, asking a person to explain personal behavior is not helpful. Try to ask "why" as little as possible. To ask "why" is frequently viewed as a challenge or advice or criticism. Advice and criticism tend to threaten people, and hence they feel less free to share. You can probably sense this by reading the examples below.

"Why don't you like him?"
"Why did you do that?"
"Why do you want to go there?"

Dealing with Feelings

In our society people generally have an easier time explaining their ideas than their feelings. Western civilization, with its emphasis upon the intellect, has taught us to ignore, distrust, or even fear our inner feelings. A large part of the art of psychotherapy in our day is helping people get in touch with their feelings—to "own" them in order to deal with them. Repressed feelings (feelings a person is unaware of at a conscious level) are at the root of many emotional difficulties. Feelings have no morality. They are neither good nor bad; they just are. It is what you do with or about your feelings that does have a moral dimension. Just having feelings (e.g. anger, fear, sexual drives) does not mean we are bad or guilty in any way. As good listeners we help people discover their inner feelings by allowing them to talk and by responding to what they say.

Sabotaged Feelings

Sometimes people trying to help others unconsciously do or say very unhelpful things when those being helped start to express real feelings. As an adult you need to be comfortable with your own emotions: crying when you are sad, yelling when you are angry, and jumping for joy when you're happy. You can see that wanting to be a helper is a real test because it challenges your own emotional growth. Only if you are relatively comfortable with your own feelings can you help another person in this area. When a person expresses his or her feelings, there are several things you should not do:

1. Don't give advice or provide a solution.
2. Don't try to make the feelings go away by offering sympathy or reassurance.
3. Don't moralize by preaching a little sermon on how the person "should" act or feel.
4. Don't warn or threaten about what will happen if the one being helped does or doesn't do something.
5. Don't lecture with facts and logic to dismiss feelings.
6. Don't judge, blame, or criticize.
7. Don't shame or ridicule.
8. Don't kid about or make light of the feelings.
9. Don't order the person to do or not do something.
10. Try not to do or say anything that will keep persons from expressing their feelings in front of you. (Don't ask them not to cry or shout or tremble.)

Keep in mind that it is very healthy for people to let out their feelings. If a person chooses to do so in front of you it means you are trusted and have provided a comfortable relationship within which this expression can occur.

By now it's probably obvious to you that the helping skills covered in this section involved a definite, somewhat predictable, process. Ideally, the process comprises the following steps:

1. The teenager needs to talk.
2. You need to listen well.
3. As the teen talks out loud, the helper acts like a mirror reflecting back what the one being helped says.
4. By talking out loud, the teenager sees his or her problem more clearly and is in better touch with personal feelings.
5. By seeing the problem and knowing his or her feelings, the teenager is better equipped to sort out options and choices that will solve the problem(s).

Three Final Cautions:

1. Don't solve problems: Remember that the helpers should not tell teenagers how to solve their problems. The answers lie within the young person buried in their feelings. They must get in touch with their feelings by talking about their situations and problems and then mustering the courage to make necessary choices and decisions for their own life. If you feel advice is appropriate, phrase it in a non-directive way—for example, "Did you ever consider...?" or "What would you think about this approach?" or "What if you...?" Avoid the following statements (and similar ones), "Why don't you...?" or "What you need to do is..." or "You should..." or "If I were you..." or "If you don't... then..."

People should have an opportunity to be responsible for their own decisions. There is a lot of satisfaction in resolving your own problems. When we are given advice we can begin to depend on outside advice, thus causing a growing feeling that we are not responsible for ourselves and that we are not capable of making decisions. Also, when others seem so capable in giving advice by making the solution sound so easy, we may begin to feel inadequate. This feeling of inadequacy creates more anxiety and defensiveness. Help that is filled with advice and that produces a dependency in the teenager is not going to serve him or her for the long run. Good guidance, in my opinion, is the gentle art of helping young people make decisions and take responsibility for those choices.

2. Don't offer false reassurance: A person feels what a person feels. While support is helpful, to rush in with reassurance tends to deny the feeling or implies that the feeling is so common that the person should not be concerned. Statements that reflect supposed "reassurance" are like the following:

"Everyone goes through that."
"That happened to me too; it will work out."
"I know how you feel."
"Don't worry about it."
"You'll be OK in a few days."

Of course we mean well when we say these and similar things. We want to help the person feel better, but the message that usually gets sent is, "You should not feel as you do." It denies the importance of the feelings and gives them little importance. Also to be avoided are "truisms" like the following (adults are notorious at dishing these out when they don't want to take the time to listen):

"Inside every cloud is a silver lining."
"Remember, nobody's perfect."
"Things take time."
"You're only human."
"It will look different tomorrow."

3. Don't counsel others beyond your capacity: If you are presented by a teenager with a serious emotional problem or situation (e.g. suicide, rape, incest, an eating disorder, sexual problems, etc.) and you feel that these are beyond your scope, don't be afraid to refer to an appropriate agency or therapist. Explain to the teenager that you will continue on the journey with him or her, but that the matter presented requires intervention and more expertise than you can provide. Recognize that the mere statement of this issue is a veiled cry for help even though the young person may try to swear you to confidentiality. Remember that you have a responsibility as a caring adult not to keep confidential threats to hurt oneself or others (like the disclosure of suicidal thoughts or eating disorders or drug addiction), signs of mental illness, and reports of physical or sexual abuse. In these circumstances you not only function as a guide, but as an advocate.

10. Faith, Doubt (and Confirmation)

When we talk about "faith" and teenagers there are two levels at which young people deal with this issue. John Westerhoff wrote a book *Will Our Children Have Faith?* and one of the main ideas in this book is that faith isn't passed on so much by some "schooling" or religious education programs as it is by a "faith-filled" community. It's us, the people in the Church, that pass it on to the children. How? By our own beliefs which they witness; through our worship together, especially sharing the Eucharist; by our actions in the world which reflect Jesus, which continue his presence among humanity. Westerhoff also says that people go through stages of faith. The young adolescent stage is getting an identity by belonging to community that has a strong identity. The older adolescent is searching more to see if the faith of this community is really his or her own. At this stage, precious beliefs and assumptions are often questioned. What I'd like to do is to look at this "Belonging" stage first and the "Searching" stage secondly. (By the way, the stage after searching is "owned" faith.)

Belonging

In the first section of this book we discussed the concept of Catholic identity in the sense of feeling a sense of belonging to a faith community. This, for a teenager, can be a crisis of faith. What do I mean?

Teenagers may have questions not so much about the existence of God but about the authenticity of the Church. If their experience of Church has been a limited one; if they don't feel welcome; if the liturgies never touch their heart; if there is no vibrant youth ministry in the parish; if there are no meaningful teenage retreats; if the parish leadership isn't cordial, doesn't know them by name; if they don't witness dedicated adults engaged in actions of mercy, advocacy and justice; if they observe the concerns of the parish to be material and self-serving; if the prayer life of the community isn't filled with the Spirit—in other words, if their experience of this community holds little meaning and they don't feel a sense of belonging (or want to belong to what they perceive to be a lifeless group), then they may not be growing in faith. They may indeed be in a Confirmation program, they may even go to a Catholic school or have attended CCD faithfully all these years. But they are more or less going through the motions. If Confirmation is a deeper initiation into the community, there has to be an experience of community first and not just an intellectual grasp of the meaning of Church.

As a sponsor or a mentoring adult, you're at least one positive dimension of the faith community. But these teenagers could be going through the motions of Confirmation preparation because of family pressure, social propriety, peer group pressure, or simply in order to get their formal religious education "over with" (and get the relatives off their back). If this is the perception of Confirmation, then you may be a clog in the wheel. But perhaps some of the challenges you offer such teenagers can be helpful. Sometimes a faith community does exist, at least at some level, but the teenagers are hesitant to really become a part. Your encouragement and support could be crucial in their entry into some meaningful church activity. Maybe the Eucharist is celebrated wonderfully but the parents of these kids never go to church and they feel strange going alone and so they never do. Maybe they can go to church with you. If you're an active parishioner, perhaps you can become an advocate for youth ministry staffing and programs. Maybe, if you're a young adult, the two of you can explore together a parish community which is alive and has a place in it for both of you.

Confirmation

Before we discuss "Searching Faith" let's talk a little bit about what Confirmation means, and I think this is helpful whether you're presently a sponsor or not. Confirmation was once a part of Baptism. In fact, in the early Church, people received Baptism, Eucharist, and Confirmation as one sacrament of initiation into the Church. Due to a lot of historical developments (which we won't go into here), the imparting of the Holy Spirit eventually became a separate rite. By the way, the "Holy Spirit" is simply the "Spirit of Jesus"—his mysterious ongoing presence in our midst. So today around the world in Roman Catholic churches we have Confirmation occurring as a separate sacrament at some age between about seven and seventeen. In the United States a pastoral custom has developed in most dioceses to celebrate Confirmation during early or late adolescence. Therefore there is an extended period of "formation" before a young Catholic enters into the fullness of initiation. I call it formation because our church documents talk about the different aspects of catechesis and youth ministry as including:

- ▶ "word" (which includes proclamation of the Gospel as well as instruction about the Catholic faith);
- ▶ worship (which includes teaching young people how to pray);
- ▶ service;
- ▶ community.

In Confirmation preparation the whole focus should not be on information but on formation. In addition to instruction, equal time and attention needs to be paid to prayer and retreats, community service, and building a sense of community and belonging. Sad to say, all too many Confirmation programs still focus almost exclusively on classroom learning.

So it's fair to say that over the years, the sacrament of Confirmation has taken on new meanings that it didn't originally have. If Baptism is entering the community in a general way, Confirmation represents a personal conviction about wanting to be connected to God (at least when it's celebrated during adolescence). It also represents a conviction about wanting to be connected with this particular faith community or parish.

Searching

Now "searching faith" occurs usually in early adulthood but can also happen during the latter part of high school. This revolves around the questioning of all childhood beliefs (like "my father or mother knows everything") and can include questioning the existence of God or Jesus. It can occur in young people who have a strong sense of belonging to a dynamic faith community as well as to those who feel little affiliation with the Church. Very often you will find that doubt about God can occur when this teenager has had to confront a tragic event at an early age (like the death of a parent, the suicide of a friend or a personal diagnosis of serious illness).

I know more about what not to do in your interaction with teenagers than I know about what to do. First of all, allow them their feelings. If they are angry at God, let them ventilate. God can take it! The Psalms in the Bible are a wonderful resource when you're mad at God. Don't deny them what they feel. It may be that they feel distanced from God, and that God doesn't care. The kingdom, the presence of God is within us, but they may just not be in touch with that right now, and that's OK. If you stand by these young persons, if you don't try to prove to them that God exists or cares, they will probably be

OK eventually. Faith is believing without seeing, without ultimate proof. It's your own faith experience that will ultimately bolster theirs if you can be with them as a gentle and patient listener. You might take the time to go through sections of the Gospel or epistles that you think might help them and suggest that they reflect on them. You might suggest a good book (like *When Bad Things Happen to Good People* by Harold Kushner). You might just pray for them because they can't pray or they can't go to Mass right now. Henri Nouwen has a beautiful definition of ministry as "the ongoing attempt to put one's own search for God, with all the moments of pain and joy, despair and hope, at the disposal of those who want to join this search but do not know how" (*Creative Ministry*, New York, Doubleday, 1971). The word compassion comes from two Latin words: *co* and *patior* which means to "suffer with." As a caring adult, as a Confirmation sponsor, your role may be simply to be there with this young person in his or her pain. It may even be that the person doesn't see Confirmation as making any sense at this point in life. And that's perfectly OK. Confirmation can be delayed; it isn't necessary to receive Confirmation for salvation. In this instance, I'd suggest you encourage the young person to discuss this with his or her parents and Confirmation program director or parish priest.

The stages of faith development are just as normal and healthy as the stages of physical and emotional growth. In fact it's usually the teenager with some depth and capacity for reflection who experiences the stages more profoundly. But each stage leads to expanded understanding and spiritual growth, and is to be acknowledged as a blessing.

Appendix:
Breaking Open the Scriptures Together

Even though this booklet isn't a "program" but hopefully an inspiration and guide for you, you might be looking for a practical strategy to serve as a conversation starter. Sometimes it's tough to start talking about spiritual matters with a teenager. And so I'm going to suggest ten sections from the Gospel which shed light on or raise questions about some important values. I'll also include a question to which you and your young person could respond, either spontaneously after reading the Scriptures or by writing your answers and then sharing what you've written. (Be sure both of you participate.)

Topic: **Charity**
Text: **Matthew 5:38–48**
Question: **Who, for you, is the "enemy"?**

Topic: **Simplicity**
Text: **Matthew 19:16–24**
Question: **What, for you, keeps you from following Jesus? Is it your wealth or something else?**

Topic: **Mercy**
Text: **Matthew 25:31–43**
Question: **How do you see yourself feeding the hungry, clothing the naked and so on?**

Topic: **Faithfulness**
Text: **Matthew 13:1-9,18-23**
Question: **What kind of "soil" do you see yourself as?**

Topic: **Prayer**
Text: **Luke 11:5-13**
Question: **Do you really believe God answers your prayer?**

Topic: **Prejudice/Compassion**
Text: **Luke 10:29-37**
(Note that Jesus and Samaritans were bitter enemies.)
Question: **Is there any group of people in society you would find it difficult to stop and help if they were in trouble? Why?**

Topic: **Trust**
Text: **Luke 12:22-32**
Question: **Do you really believe God takes care of you? How?**

Topic: **Death**
Text: **Luke 12:35-48**
Question: **Do you feel ready to meet God if you should die suddenly?**

Topic: **Forgiveness**
Text: **Luke 15:11-32**
Question: **How do you feel about this story? Is forgiveness difficult for you?**

Topic: **Beatitudes**
Text: **Matthew 5:1-12**
Question: **If these lines are a summary of the Christian lifestyle, which beatitude do you feel you need to assume more in your life?**